SandCastle™

Math Made Fun

Let's All Assume, We Can Measure Volume!

Tracy Kompelien

Consulting Editors, Diane Craig, M.A./Reading Specialist
and Susan Kosel, M.A. Education

ABDO
Publishing Company

Published by ABDO Publishing Company, 4940 Viking Drive, Edina, Minnesota 55435.

Printed in the United States.

Credits
Edited by: Pam Price
Curriculum Coordinator: Nancy Tuminelly
Cover and Interior Design and Production: Mighty Media
Photo Credits: BananaStock Ltd., Brand X Pictures, Comstock, Photodisc, ShutterStock, Stockbyte, Wewerka Photography

Library of Congress Cataloging-in-Publication Data

Kompelien, Tracy, 1975-
    Let's all assume, we can measure volume! / Tracy Kompelien.
        p. cm. -- (Math made fun)
    ISBN 10 1-59928-535-5 (hardcover)
    ISBN 10 1-59928-536-3 (paperback)

    ISBN 13 978-1-59928-535-1 (hardcover)
    ISBN 13 978-1-59928-536-8 (paperback)
    1. Volume (Cubic content)--Juvenile literature. 2. Area measurement--Juvenile literature. I. Title.

QC104.K66 2007
516'.156--dc22

                                                                    2006021578

SandCastle Level: Transitional

SandCastle™ books are created by a professional team of educators, reading specialists, and content developers around five essential components—phonemic awareness, phonics, vocabulary, text comprehension, and fluency—to assist young readers as they develop reading skills and strategies and increase their general knowledge. All books are written, reviewed, and leveled for guided reading, early reading intervention, and Accelerated Reader® programs for use in shared, guided, and independent reading and writing activities to support a balanced approach to literacy instruction. The SandCastle™ series has four levels that correspond to early literacy development. The levels help teachers and parents select appropriate books for young readers.

Emerging Readers
(no flags)

Beginning Readers
(1 flag)

Transitional Readers
(2 flags)

Fluent Readers
(3 flags)

These levels are meant only as a guide. All levels are subject to change.

Volume is
the amount that
a container holds.

Words used to
describe volume:

cup   **quart**
gallon   **tablespoon**
pint   **teaspoon**

three
3

This is **one** gallon.

There is a of milk

in our .

There are 4
quarts **in 1** gallon.

This is a quart.

We buy a of juice at the store.

juice at the store.

There are 4 cups in 1 quart.

This is a pint. We whip a of cream to put on our .

There are 2 pints in 1 quart.

This is one cup. I eat a

of for a snack.

There are 2 cups
in 1 pint.

This is a tablespoon. Dad uses one ⟍◯ of oil when he makes 🥞.

There are 16 tablespoons in 1 cup.

This is a teaspoon. Mom gives me one ⟶ of when I am sick.

There are 3 teaspoons in 1 tablespoon.

Let's All Assume, We Can Measure Volume!

Valerie and Tina have a lemonade stand. In the hot summer, lemonade is in demand.

Two quarts of water
fill the pitcher up.
They sell the lemonade
for 50 cents a cup.

They sell eight cups
and that is the end.
Till they get two more
quarts and fill it again!

Measuring Volume Every Day!

When I make cookies,

I use two cups of flour.

eighteen
18

After playing outside,
I make sure I drink one
quart of water.

I use two tablespoons of hot chocolate mix to make hot cocoa.

Which container can hold the most?

Comparison Chart

gallon   quart   pint   cup   tablespoon   teaspoon

1 gallon							
1 quart		1 quart		1 quart		1 quart	
1 pint	1 pint	1 pint	1 pint	1 pint	1 pint	1 pint	1 pint
1 cup	1 cup	1 cup	1 cup	1 cup	1 cup	1 cup	1 cup	1 cup	1 cup	1 cup	1 cup	1 cup	1 cup	1 cup	1 cup

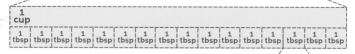

1 cup															
1 tbsp	1 tbsp	1 tbsp	1 tbsp	1 tbsp	1 tbsp	1 tbsp	1 tbsp	1 tbsp	1 tbsp	1 tbsp	1 tbsp	1 tbsp	1 tbsp	1 tbsp	1 tbsp

1 gallon = 4 quarts, 8 pints, or 16 cups

1 quart = 2 pints or 4 cups

1 pint = 2 cups

1 cup = 16 tablespoons

1 tablespoon = 3 teaspoons

1 tbsp		
1 tsp	1 tsp	1 tsp